ENTERING

ENTERING

SAPPHO

poetry by

SARAH DOWLING

Coach House Books, Toronto

first edition

 Canada Council Conseil des Arts
for the Arts du Canada

 ONTARIO ARTS COUNCIL
CONSEIL DES ARTS DE L'ONTARIO
an Ontario government agency
un organisme du gouvernement de l'Ontario

Canadä

Published with the generous assistance of the Canada Council for the Arts
and the Ontario Arts Council. Coach House Books also acknowledges the
support of the Government of Canada through the Canada Book Fund and
the Government of Ontario through the Ontario Book Publishing Tax Credit.

LIBRARY AND ARCHIVES CANADA CATALOGUING IN PUBLICATION

Title: Entering Sappho / poetry by Sarah Dowling.
Names: Dowling, Sarah, 1982- author.
Identifiers: Canadiana (print) 20200294318 | Canadiana (ebook)
20200294334 | ISBN 9781552454183 (softcover) | ISBN 9781770566514
(EPUB) | ISBN 9781770566521 (PDF)
Subjects: LCGFT: Poetry.
Classification: LCC PS8607.O9875 E58 2020 | DDC C811/.6—dc23

Entering Sappho is available as an ebook: ISBN 978 1 77056 651 4 (EPUB),
ISBN 978 1 77056 652 1 (PDF)

To a future time

TABLE OF CONTENTS

POSSESSION SOUND

CLIP

Monday, May 15, Sappho, WA –
a logging chapter is closed. Those

country maidens were good riders,
flowers blooming in an old bathtub,

cows grazing in an orchard. Garments
wet as they should be. Across the dirt

road, peasant girls on the front porch,
a town of five houses – oh, anyone

would want
to live

in the fenced area nearby. Anyone,
wet dress around her feet.

Her dress about her ankles, an old
bathtub. In the front yard, horses

munch grass. What wench, country-
fried at the side of the highway, has

electricity, television, a telephone – oh,
it's for the birds! What rustic girl

plans to enter her prize quarter-
horse in races this summer? She's

never known anything but logging
trucks, she doesn't even draw her

gown across her feet.

Water flowers bloom. Country girls
turn north at Sappho, go to Pysht,

spend time darning holes in wool
socks and wondering, why would

anyone pull rags
over her ankles?

What girl wants to live in nearness
to fishing? What country girl is un-

spoiled nature?

Young mothers by choice, they
hear about it three days later. They

still don't pull the cloth over
their feet.

Down Highway 101 a piece, what
country girl says you can do these

things in cities, small-town life is
all I want to know? They front on

the old houses for truckers and
tourists, tearing down the last

of the company shacks. What
girl waits like a wife for wet

attackers, spinning yarns from
her country dress? Oh,

that girl gathers it up with artless
grace. You can still see a girl's feet

at Sappho. You can see the owner
of the company store.

Those girls would sit, eating clams.
Soft blossoms, simple dresses

in a line on the ground. Maybe
loggers and their families shot

deer, bear, elk – some
girl in the area.

Why would anyone want to live
when May 1 the post office closes

forever? Those girls lay claim to
time. Backward and forward, their

hemlines sweeping the ground.

ENTERING SAPPHO

ORAL HISTORY

She was reading a book, I think it was.
She was a Greek, I don't know or I don't

remember. It was in a play, or well no,
she's one of the characters. But anyway,

her name was Sappho. Oh. So, they was
building the old place over here, and the

store, and the hotel, and you get the post
office, so they named that Sappho. So

that's where Sappho was originally named,
how it got its name – reading that book.

You're ENTERING
Ninety-seven Troys
Eighty-three Eurekas
Fifty-seven Etnas
Fifty-six Antiochs
Fifty-four Athenses
Fifty-four Romes
Fifty-one Albions
And fifty Arcadias

Forty-nine Palmyras
Forty-eight Spartas
Forty-five Senecas
Thirty-nine Phoenixes
Thirty-nine Alphas
Thirty-seven Homers
Thirty-six Caledonias
Thirty-six Carthages
Thirty-five Macedonias
Thirty-three Uticas
And thirty-one Corinths

Thirty Milos
Twenty-nine Omegas
Twenty-seven Smyrnas
Twenty-five Argoses
Twenty-five Adrians
And twenty-four Olympias

Right here, over here just a little ways,
about a hundred feet the other side of

you. This is Sappho. That ain't Sappho
down there. This is the town site here.

There's one block over there, and one
here, and another one down below. And

one time here we had a saloon and a paper
and a hotel and a grocery and a livery barn.

When did they come out here, your in-laws?
I think about '93, '92 or 3, I think it was.

They built the store first, I suppose. Yeah,
the store was out front, the hall was up

over, and then the buildings and the dining
rooms and the rooms was upstairs. And the

attic. And that building was just about a
hundred feet the other side of the house

here? I think about, yeah. Toward the
highway? I'll be damned. It stood till –

it stood till it all fell down. I guess about
1900 and 38, something-thirty along there,

just went down. And that was all.

Well did they have the hotel at the same
time as they had the store? Yes, it was all

built together. All built together, and the
hall too. What did they use the hall for,

other than dances? Well, in the wintertime
they used to use it to dry clothes, mostly.

It had a big mangle up there, a drying
mangle, they used to mangle the clothes

and sheets and everything. You mangle
them – now, you didn't have electricity?

No. Just rolls about that big around and
about that long.

But there was no heat on it. No, there was
no heat. No, you have to have them dry

when you mangle them. You'd say it was
about two feet long? Yeah, about that, yeah.

I've never run across that. Then, how much
would they charge for a night's lodging?

Seventy-five cents. Did that include any
meals, or was that just – Your supper and

breakfast and your bed. Well, I'll be darned.

You're ENTERING
Twenty-three Akrons
Twenty-three Clios
And twenty-two Venuses

Twenty-one Delphis and Delphoses
Twenty-one Altamonts
Twenty-one Cambrias
Twenty Catos
Twenty Ionias
And twenty Ovids

Twenty Pomonas
Nineteen Hectors
Eighteen Orions
Eighteen –adelphias
Eighteen Marses
Eighteen Urbanas
Seventeen Altas, Atlos, and Altuses
Seventeen Sardises
Seventeen Solons
Seventeen Atticas
Seventeen Cincinnatis
Seventeen Euclids
And sixteen Platos

In fact, we lived there, we was married
the first day of January in 1901, and six

or seven years we lived down in the prairie,
why we lived there practically all the time.

The prairie down here, they were down
here first. They started that before there

was any Sappho. Yeah. When they moved
it up here, then they kept the name. Oh, I

see. I think my wife's come back.

Oh, hi. How are you? Doing good. Make
another excursion? This is my wife, Sylvia.

How do you do? I see you've got the daily
plate there. Yeah. You were saying about

the post office? Did you have a post office
here? Oh yes, we had a post office. That was

The Sappho Post Office.

You're ENTERING
Sixteen Virgils
Fifteen Atlases
Fifteen Scipios
Fourteen Syracuses
And thirteen Ciceros

Thirteen Vestas
Thirteen Neros
Twelve Sylvanias
Twelve Albas and Albias
Twelve Cerescos and Crescos
Twelve Marathons
Twelve Xenias
Eleven Fabiuses
And eleven Utopias

Eleven Bereas
Eleven Cereses
Eleven Cretes
Eleven Hibernias
Ten Neptunes
Ten Scios
Ten Aeolias and Eolias
Ten Corydons
And ten Jupiters

We had two or three cows. Used to create
a lot of rutabagas and cabbages for the

cows, things like that. Did your mother-
in-law do the cooking for the hotel, I

suppose? Yeah, she and my wife. A lot of
work there. Yeah, well it was. We was over

here the time that my son was born. We had
thirty-two there that night, just my mother-

in-law and my wife and I and all that crowd
and my kid coming along about five o'clock

in the morning.

They had quite a little thing going out there
on the beach out there, Taylor Point. That

was Strawberry Point we used to call that
down there. Yeah. Yeah, I haven't got it

quite straight yet now. They changed. They
call different places different things. Yeah.

Well since the Coast Guard has come in
they patrol the beaches and trails. They

renamed all them points and stuff, yeah.
It isn't quite the same.

SOFT MEMORY

Because so soon as I see you – a cold
sweat spreads all over my body – it

has stolen all directions – sweat pours
from my body – a buzzing noise in my

ears – a cold sweat floods me – a cold
sweat floods me, and I'm greener than

grass – and I feel like dying. Sweat
gets on me – and close, half-raised

I lie down in the grass, a subtle flame
flowing in my veins – what would

kiss

    your knees –

a cold sweat floods me – a trembling
seizes me entirely – a subtle fire runs

in me – a faltering, subtle fire starts
running under my skin – a subtle fire,

a tremor through me fully, that short
fire is under my skin – it seems

to me –

Because so soon as I see you I become
still – subtle fire slips into my veins –

my tongue is silent – hardly I saw you
on the edge of my lips – my muffled

voice – and I'm down

                like the

                          grass

of the field

as soon as I see you – hardly because I'
ve seen you and I lack the voice – this

voice no longer reaches my lips and
my eyes perceive nothing – I'm green-

er than grass – and I die almost of fail-
ure – I trickle with sweat – it seems okay

I'm not afraid – sweat shakes me whole –
I listen close – your voice and your laugh

I listen close, okay I'm

                    vibrating songs –

Because as soon as I see you, a sweat
of agony bathes me – and a whole trem-

bling seizes me, and a fever diffuses
under my skin – I'm sitting right in

front of you. I'm without breath and
without movement – as soon as I see

you breathing fails me, I'm entirely
fire, and I envy –

and

we must dare all –

okay, this trembling seized me – your
laugh – okay there's fire in my skin,

droning in my ears – I hear your voice
so sweet and indistinct – as soon as I

see you it seized me – seized me as
soon –

Because so soon as I see you – the en-
chanting disorder – I cannot speak, eyes

fixed on you – I think – I hit – I enter –
gently, I

       dare all –

          but

listen, my ears are ringing – my eyes
continue, in a moment I'm blurred – I'm

covered – I'm thick clouds – at once I miss
my voice and my tongue breaks, my ears

ring – I drip

        I turn green, I'm grass – and
I come like the prairie – okay, this fever

burns me and it seems that finally I did
live

You're ENTERING
Nine Ithacas
Nine Ulysseses
Nine Argentas and Argentums
Nine Helvetias
Nine Rhodeses
Nine Tullys
Nine –sylvanias
Eight Elysians and Elysiums
And eight Rubicons

Eight Agricolas
Eight Ajaxes
Eight Deltas
Eight Marcelluses
Eight Pellas
Seven Arguses
Seven Aurelias and Aureliuses
Seven Bucyruses
Seven Castors
Seven Laconias
Seven Castalias
Seven Manliuses
And seven Mentors

More than a movement – I shiver, my
ears hear – I can't find expressions –

it seems – I hear you talk – it's sweet,
I listen to your words – smile, listen

close – it's nothing, it's subtle, just a
little fire under my heart, my chest, my

eyes, my skin

                 – it's like

                            the buzzing of a
bee, okay –

my whole body shivers – confused sing-
ing buzzing – my ears – my face, all liv-

ing grass, all breeze and dew – my sight
and my ears ringing off and in my mad-

ness – I become

More than a movement, I'm greener,
I'm grass pushed down – okay – I'm

running speechless – green-pale and
ringing. I'm vein and fire – I tremble,

okay – I hardly breathe – I'm in you –

                I breathe –

okay

– I'm close –
            I'm – covered with clouds.

My sweating tongue – my heart beats
faster – my throat – and we

                        resign our
selves to all –

More than a movement – more green-
pale than grass, it seems to me that –

there, my ears are ringing – my eyes
are covered with clouds – I tremble

and – my eyes no longer see – it seems
that I will die – cold sweat, tongue chain-

ed – my ears – I cannot think of any
more words – my tongue is broken –

my tongue stops, I – hit enter – my
body in a cold sweat – sound cannot

escape my throat, making me feel all
these possessions – crazy anxiety

squeezes my

                     come –

I'm greener than grass – my heart beats
faster, my tongue is broken –

You're ENTERING
Seven Mount Idas
Six Bonos
Six Bovinas
Six Coronas
And six Didos

Six Elyrias
Six Hesperias and Hesperuses
Six Pactoluses
Six Romuluses
Six Ilions and Iliums
Six Lithias
Six Petras and Petroses
Six Stixes and Styxes
And six Vulcans

Five Galateas and Galatias
Five Galens
Five Hannibals
Five Medias
Five Athenas and Athenias
Five Brutuses
Five Cadmuses
Five Caesars
Five Ephesuses
And five Nestors

Sitting in front of you, I'm greener than
grass, I can't say a word, my ears are

ringing – I sweat to hear you and see
you laugh – in a way, I turned pale –

my breathing stops, my eyes no longer
see, it seems I'm

            going to die – no, my

whole
      body shivers,

               my eyes don't –
nothing –

     it made me

faint, just – this trembling seized me
 – and the hurts rushed entirely from

my heart – my chest is this smile that
keeps coming off me, this beating

of my heart, what happiness swells –

a fire surges through me – I seem –
okay, no

Sitting in front of you, I can only ex-
press what – look in vain for words –

my ears are ringing – no, it makes me
jump – what, even a word – I shiver

so pleasant, I'm barely breathing –

pallor decorates my face, my ears don't
hear – a cold sweat seizes me – my tongue

is ice –

      my broken tongue –

it seems okay – I sweat – it melts, it
runs down my ears – and when I see

you – at the moment of my throat your
laugh melts too, my heart – not a sound

– no, a quiet sweat floods me and I hear
your voice and watch your lips flourish

this joy – for what

Sitting in front of you – deep into this
– I say it's okay – being alone and

away from you there's this charm caus-
ing trouble – there's this trembling,

paler than the withered grass – well,
what – would

he

– no,

I'm nearly dead – what would he know –
– my heart goes crazy – who can sit – who

can hear you talk – no, that morning the
meadow's pallor invaded my – no, that

morning trembling seized me – no, you
barely play – this time – no – this view

too delectable – this weakness – we've
got to – no, it's motionless – no, I'm al-

ways watching – no – I'm wandering
at the side of the road

You're ENTERING
One Sappho, only
One Sappho, just this
One Sappho,

just pull over.

NEOCLASSICAL PLACE NAMES
of
NORTH AMERICA

THIS WORD: I WANT

Tell us about the Mediterranean realm and
the visions of their American patrons. Tell us
about the hollow peak of Mt. Olympus, and
the frontier by which we exceed it. In these

ancient and modern times, we've done so many
things. Teach us about the thick swarm of gods
and the fifty Albions, our own kleptographic
hands, and our vicious greed for beauty.

Teach us to believe that these names
were plucked from our best dormant traits,
pulled from a belt of elusive gods who personify
the evening. Teach us to run our snow fingers

down the valleys of blue waste. Show us how
to lap the warm, wet edges of Possession Sound.

In our period of birth and consolidation, daughter
colonies spread outward, open. We have recorded
2,405 classical names scoring the rocks, pounding
the flanks of these northern peripheral zones.

A rural settlement pattern, a belt in the shape
of a bent isosceles. This migration front is
thick with fresh adoptions: we're filling in
the holes. We are a pattern of blotches across

this uniform nutrient medium. Aurum, Cyprum,
Eureka, college towns bravely christened Exotica
decorate these resinous slopes and mountain
basins. A zodiac of ancient characters

documents our extroverted buoyancy, our
scatter over soft and bushy lands.

Mythological personages supplement lively
post offices. What they most resemble is a pan-
theon of hungry dogs. What they most resemble
is an advanced stage of a bacterial culture. What

we most resemble is the end of the world.
We are conspicuous, we pluck the strings
of historical association and make another
exclusion. We are a winnowing, a slow tick

of the intellectual pacemaker, a growing edge.
Wait till they get up close. This movement
happened in more than one hundred cities:
Agricola, Bovina, Pomona, Marathon, Akron,

Ajax, Salix, and others extending in a long line
below the wet cloud blanket.

This terrible red gash was
turning red like

it was forgotten, like the pluckers
forgot, somehow – the pickers

forgot it, the harvesters missed
or forgot somehow, and your

vision dimmed with
tears, with it reddening

high at the tip but you
missed it, being out of

reach you didn't notice, rather,
you did notice, but the

apple-pickers forgot, you
missed it – the pluckers

forgot it. No, you didn't
miss it – no, not forgot

We plot and interpret the practice of memorial-
izing some imagined ancient world. We place
symbols on the map. Postdate archaic expansions
so that their margins in time, space, and information

become concerning. We place the weight of the
heavens on our shoulders and don a principal
belt of plantation agriculture. Trace a triangle
with its apex east of Syracuse and call it a foray

into terra incognita. Hang cities like blue scalloped
veils: Eros in Louisiana and Arizona, Troys to lose
for a kiss, convulsive surges forward as traits
of national character. We cultivate some vulnerable

spot on our bodies and establish towns for heartbreak:
the old Greek's strait, the inland sea, the wild peninsula.

The nonlocal nature of our naming is a mouse-
trap, an arrangement of symbols. It's how we learn
what guns are for. It's that subconscious, inarticulate
feeling of being flanked to the west and the south

by history in the following equation: those who
existed over those who expired. We have a good
many departments examining the hearth of our
epoch, the stages of the cycle, the occupation

and preemption in which we deem our worst traits
dormant, gone, a disappeared doctrine. We bear
witness to our own peculiar styles, study the forested
shores of our own importance, the way we ram

each other and sail on, changing shaggy green
to soft blue.

This terrible red gash
across your face was turning

red high on the tip of my
lips it was reddening up-

on the top-most branch,
it was reddening, red-

dening on the highest
blush like a delicate flame

reddens your skin, like the
honeyapple turning red

on the high branch,
ripening and turning

red on the – reddening high
on the – getting ripe like

that sweet apple on the top-
most bough

US

You may forget but I remember well one day how
thrilled I was when I took little Annie Schofield

by the hand, a blood-red rose flaming with all the
long-buried passions of the South. I had many dolls,

but my favourite was a lady in a red dress. I helped
her along from rock to rock in the shallow water

at the river's edge. In the pale Gothic garden there
bursts something you may forget but our minds

worked overtime on what we would like to have.
After a great deal of coaxing, I called her my little

red girl. You may forget but occasionally the law
has its revenge, and I had been promised. The

intoxicating odour had become a delicate perfume.
You may forget but I remember well the shallow

water, the river's edge, how thrilled I was when I
helped her by the hand, took her along from rock to

rock, little red-haired Annie Schofield there. How
I was flaming, a blood-red rose.

Think of Dor, who was a big strong boy. You may
forget but I had been promised a pair of boots which

were to come by mail from Tacoma. I had been
promised roses of Lesbos which turned a pallid

pink, and you may forget but my brother Elmer was
to bring them from Pysht, and I waited on the river-

bank dancing up and down and hollering with the
long-buried possessions of the South. With the

children and their dolls. You may forget but in the
pale Gothic gardens, my pretty little boots budded

and bloomed and withered all unseen, or seen
by but a single eye. You may forget but my pretty

boots proved to be a pair of men's No. 9 shoes in
which I might have lost myself. You may forget

but pale lilies of fancy, passionate roses of desire
blossomed there.

Let me tell you that I might have lost myself. Let
me tell you about this terrible red gash across my

face. You may forget but Mr. Gorder, who was
youthful and spry in spite of his long red beard,

was cruising out of his claim one day. He lay silent
but breathing, unconscious, and with his big .44

strapped to his side. You may forget but Dor was
a big strong boy, and let me tell you this about the

long-buried passions of the Sound. Let me tell you
about their intoxicating odour which becomes a deli-

cate perfume. Let me tell you, I had many dolls but
my favourite was a lady in a red dress and I called her

my little rose of Lesbos. Let me tell you how she
turned a pallid pink, and then bloomed and withered

all unseen. The children coloured red boots, they came
by mail from Tacoma. The children coloured that up.

With all the long-buried passions of the South,
red roses of desire blossom. I had many dolls,

but my favourite was the pale lilies of fancy, the
passionate blood-lady in a red dress. Someone

in some future time will think that I helped her
along from rock to rock in the shallow water at the

river's edge, a little red girl who was to come
this way from Tacoma. In the pale Gothic garden

I had been promised three bursts, something. Some-
one and some future. You may forget but our minds

worked overtime on what we would like to have.

You may forget that one day with my little red
girl in my pretty red boots when they came

by mail from Tacoma. I had been cruising out
of my claim, I had been promised roses of Lesbos,

I had turned a pallid pink, I had been promised a
beard. I was youthful and spry in spite of this, and

you may forget but my brother Elmer was to bring
me dolls, which I would dash on the rocks. After a

great deal of coaxing, someone in some future time
will call this my little red fancy, my passionate edge.

You may forget but occasionally the pretty boots
have their revenge, and I had been promised. Mr.

Gorder, who was from Pysht, and I waited for some
future children. I thought of them on the riverbank,

dancing up and down. Their delicate breathing,
their intoxicating .44.

I lay silent but breathing, unconscious, and let me
tell you this – this big Gothic rose was strapped to

my side. Let me tell you that I might have lost my-
self. Let me tell you about my favourite, who was

wearing a dress and pretty little boots, my pretty
red boots. Let me tell you this – I had been prom-

ised. Let me tell you how I rocked her in the shallow
red of the river water. Someone in some future

time will think how thrilled I was. Someone in
some future time will think we lay silent but

breathing, that my favourite was unconscious.
You may forget that I'm a big strong boy, you

forget that I had many dolls. Let me tell you this
about long-buried possession, let me tell you about

the sound. I waited among red lilies, hollering and
strapped with this, a big .44 at my side.

You may forget but I had been promised a pale
Gothic garden. I had been promised a lot of blood.

I had budded and bloomed. I had possessed men's
boots. I had lost myself. You may forget but some-

one in some future time will think of my pale lilies
of fancy, my red roses of desire. I might have been

Gothic, I might have burst blood, I might have
flamed a rose at Annie with this terrible red gash

across her face. You may forget but someone in some
future time will think of Mr. Gorder. He was youth-

ful and spry in spite of his long red claim. He was
cruising out with his beard one day, and then withered

all unseen. In the shallow water at the river's edge,
let me tell you – that red gash. Let me tell you,

we were children. Let me tell you what we coloured.

Let me tell you about this intoxicating odour. Let me
tell you how she was to bring me. I had many dolls

but my favourite was a dewy riverbank, and I called her
my little unconscious, and I called her my wet prairie.

Let me tell you how I helped her blossom by the hand.
Let me tell you about the roses, let me tell you about

Lesbos, where we lay silent but breathing, pallid and
pink. Let me tell you how I was strapped to her side.

After a great deal of coaxing I called her and then
bloomed, I called her and then withered. I called her

all unseen.

Someone in some future time will think I took
little Annie Schofield by the hand. Someone

in some future time will think of the pale Gothic
gardens, the terrible gash across her, blood-red.

Someone in some future time will think of how
our minds worked, unconscious. How after a great

deal of breathing, we lay silent and called for a
little future. In some red time, someone will think

of how my brother Elmer was to bring me from
Pysht. I waited on the riverbank hollering up and

down. I was dancing, a big doll strapped to my side.
I had many .44s, and with my favourite I thought

occasionally of possession, of what I would most
like to have. Someone in some pale Gothic garden

will think of me and bloom, someone will think of me
and burst, someone will think of our time as a blood-

rose, flaming with long-buried passions, flaming
with possession, flaming at Annie, flaming right

where I lost myself.

LEUCADIAN LEAP

ORNAMENT

If someone had hair bound with purple instruments
If someone had hair bound with beautiful practice
If someone had hair bound with accurate grass

If someone had hair bound with known targets
If someone had hair bound with red testimonies
If someone had hair bound with black stones

If someone had hair bound with present possession
If someone had hair bound with archipelagoes
If someone had hair bound with the asking moon

If someone had hair bound with soft rivers
If someone had hair bound with target affect
If someone had hair bound with older friends

If someone had hair bound with a dead revolver
If someone had hair bound with heavier limbs
If someone had hair bound with plinking seas

If someone had hair bound with dead ports
If someone had hair bound with a convenient will
If someone had hair bound with rosy fingers

If someone had hair bound with a pistol moon
If someone had hair bound with smokeless gulfs
If someone had hair bound with bays and knives

If someone had hair bound with convenient lands
If someone had hair bound with the jacketed earth
If someone had hair bound with present power

If someone had hair bound with smokeless hands
If someone had hair bound with beautiful possession
If someone had hair bound with rounds of sleep

If someone had hair bound with lay branches
If someone had hair bound with special accuracy
If someone had hair bound with the convenient moon

If someone had hair bound with practice rocks
If someone had hair bound with heavier trees
If someone had hair bound with willed velocity

If someone had hair bound with applications
If someone had hair bound with erect beaches
If someone had hair bound with all this grass

If someone had hair bound with willing fields
If someone had hair bound with possessive limbs
If someone had hair bound with a state sword

If someone had hair bound with the expedition
If someone had hair bound with laying witness
If someone had hair bound with contradiction

If someone had hair bound with martial rounds
If someone had hair bound with my unwilling self
If someone had hair bound with point muskets

If someone had hair bound with knives and seas
If someone had hair bound with black plinking
If someone had hair bound with continuous stones

If someone had hair bound with target rounds
If someone had hair bound with artful practice
If someone had hair bound with a lay cross

If someone had hair bound with great inscriptions
If someone had hair bound with black possession
If someone had hair bound with naked trees

If someone had hair bound with a given pistol
If someone had hair bound with the endless present
If someone had hair bound with soft memorials

If someone had hair bound with bulky pens
If someone had hair bound with knives' targets
If someone had hair bound with a pile of limbs

If someone had hair bound with the following testimonial
If someone had hair bound with friends' weapons
If someone had hair bound with soft powder

If someone had hair bound with accurate property
If someone had hair bound with practice power
If someone had hair bound with a semi-cross

If someone had hair bound with chamber accuracy
If someone had hair bound with soft applications
If someone had hair bound with beautiful things

If someone had hair bound with neighbouring lands
If someone had hair bound with sapphic history
If someone had hair bound in a big mangle

THESE THINGS NOW FOR MY COMPANIONS /
I SHALL SING BEAUTIFULLY

Be it known that I carried a revolver, a willing
pistol, into this century. I had an interesting name,

after all. I was Troy, Eureka, Etna, and Antioch.
I scraped a big red gash. I was terrible but I for-

got. I took the older-than-being knives to beauti-
ful limbs. I named myself for the ancient poet-

ess. I called out to Athens, Rome, Albion, and
Arcadia. I thought the pluckers would forget all

the worst parts

of me. I wrote, rosy-fingered in smokeless powder.
Few people in the area were aware. In forty-nine

Palmyras, forty-eight Spartas, forty-five Senecas,
and thirty-nine Phoenixes I penned a dead practice,

I converted my models to local names. All this I
harvested, missed, and forgot somehow – my

vision dimmed with tears. I pulled over. I was at
the side

of the highway. I took a clipper through Possess-
ion Sound. I moved the stones so they would give

in. They moved in appointment when I walked in
possession, when I walked in possession of these

territories. I took the trees, I erected a cross by
beaches. I moved within and without in a sign

of possession, taking fields and trees, taking grass
and branches, with a ship's martial secretary and

weapons behind me. I brought on heavier sleep, I
willed all to black. I said –

come lie down in Sappho –
dress a little whiter and pres

                           ent

your wants – everything is a
wet curtain everything is a wind
blowing – pull the coun

                         try open

spread the night flat – stack
paper further down the pave
ment – every

                 thing west is a

platform another clock a set
of widening walls

I carried the name of the family that settled
these thirty-three Uticas and thirty-one Cor-

inths, twenty-nine Omegas, twenty-seven
Smyrnas and remade the coming century. I

was reddening high at the tip. I tangled my
hair. I pumped rounds into convenient targets.

I took what I could. I carried a spreading pat-
tern of blotches. I carried all that fire

with me. I dreamed of twenty-four Olympias,
twenty-three Clios, and twenty-two Venuses who

were all fond of Sappho's poetry. I ran across
beaches, they didn't notice. Rather, they did

but I took the heavier revolvers. In Akron, in
Delphi, in Altamont, and Cambria, the apple-

pickers missed me. I was smokeless, amusingly
soft. In twenty Catos, twenty Ionias, and twenty

Ovids, nineteen Hectors, and eighteen Orions,
I told a little story about how I surpassed what

I entered. I plucked. I touched that special
accuracy of power. I plucked seventeen Solons,

seventeen Atticas, seventeen Cincinnatis, seven-
teen Euclids, Platos, Virgils, and Ciceros. I was

plinking in this terrible somehow. I gashed my
own face, high at the lips. I thought I was subtle.

I was on the top-most branch. I lay down. I
said –

present the west and every
thing's sexual – a country
a clock an

            other curtain a
spreading pavement – you
can't do it when every

                      thing
is so much further and mission
time enters every hit –
blowing paper get

                  ting wet
getting night – can't think of
anything that moves can't
think of any

                thing whiter can't
stack it all up

I took possession of these lands and the neigh-
bouring seas, rivers, ports, gulfs, archipelagoes,

and this bay, and this bay, and this bay. I sucked
up what is sunk under the black earth. I take and

took possession of all the things that belong here,
that I might take possession of more lands, take

possession of the neighbouring seas, take possess-
ion of the black rivers, and the bay, the port, the

gulf, and these sheets of water. All this I affirmed

publicly. I testified to it. I made all these hurts,
I became a mangle. I thought I was subtle. I said

it was our world, I said our world was youth.
I said these were our places, I said what we had

was heat. I went, I touched down, a soft flame.
A same-old same-old Sappho, a little-different

thing. I, the secretary, and I, the commander of
my own expedition, entered Sylvanias through to

Albas. I targeted a mangle of friends. I said –

can't right every tipping plat-
form
 – everything sex
                    ual's always
further west – everything blow
ing down – dress with no walls
no cur
          tain no night – nothing
west of Sappho rain and you're
present in a country a time a
stack
          ed invasion – you're spread
ing out pulling wants – getting
wet getting whiter

I take and I took a large cross on my should-
ers. I arranged it in martial order, with my

muskets and other arms. I was willing to hit
limbs, to be new. I named eleven Utopias, el-

even Cretes, and eleven Hibernias. I took the
state to have a case, a thing like a black, new

will-to-power. I carried this in procession, in
possession. I was the honeyapple of Ithaca. I

was a special kind

of Elysium. That being concluded, I placed the
cross and erected a pile of stones. At the foot of it,

a soft memorial and a sign. I was a new century
revolver. All of these seas and lands and districts,

continuous and contiguous to myself. I entered
eight Deltas, seven Aurelias, Didos, and all my

seven Mentors. I just went down, and that was it.
I rang the bell, I wrang my hands. I said –

pull right out of everything
– you see it blow

                 ing you're
wet paper you're a curtain
flat and white – hit the lights
in

  vade the present – undress
the country night its hard rain
its width and length in time –
Sappho is want

               ing everything
twice as west – you have the
mission can't think what we're
here for

I was ripening. I was turning red. I was that sweet
Ida on the top-most bough. But somehow there

was this terrible gash and I couldn't reach it.
Many things rushed and fell, another and another.

I stripped bare a tree and made a cross. I placed
on it these words: forever be it known to all those

to whom the present testimonial, instrument, or letter
of possession comes: this naked cross, which is the

tree is given the following title and the following
inscription:

We thought we were beautiful. Thought we
were different beings. We just mangled every-

thing, mangled ourselves as we went in, rush-
ing. We made the news, another end. A soft yes

as we fled into it. Things were different till
they fell. Things were tangled where they lay

down. We stood for the hurts we called becoming.
We fell, and all these places hurt for heat. We rushed

down to the bushes. We all rushed our excursion.
We thought we were the flame of youth. We thought

we were the soft sweet grass. We were big but we
were only flames. We thought that was beautiful

but the heat mangled things. We made a few places
to call each other. We made a place to lay our

youth. We made it hurt. We went down, just
down. We fell. Yes, this is how it ended: fire

at the side of the highway. Dead rivers, smoky
skies. Jets trailing overhead. What we stood for

wasn't much. We all rushed out to see it. Our world
is just a big burn, a bush grown over. But now our

hair is down. The grass is wet. The grass grows
back. All we have is this thicker becoming, all

we are is this tangled perhaps.

Entering Sappho is a portal into history – the bits that are meant to be meaningful to a person like me, as well as those that are repugnant. Entering Sappho is taking on a series of voices, versions of the ancient poetess and traces of the town. Entering Sappho is addressing history and its daughter colony, the present.

Entering Sappho is a silly ritual. When you're driving to the coast on Highway 101, you come to the sign, stop, and take a picture. Entering Sappho is how you pay tribute to the original lesbian and to the generations of queers who've also paused here to photograph themselves. Entering Sappho is a moment of gleeful excitement. Cars zoom past, going much faster than seems possible. It's a little scary, but entering Sappho is also hilarious. Picture the hand gestures, how people pose, decade after decade, in front of this unwitting monument.

Entering Sappho is digging into the history of a settlement founded in 1895, just before the garbage-dump discovery of the papyrus versions of Sappho's poems. This is a town with few textual traces, without any standing physical remnant. Entering Sappho is reading the slim, self-published memoirs of former child-settlers, their fantastical memories of running through the forest, their naive recollections of who was armed and who was bleeding. Entering Sappho is listening to the oral histories held in the Special Collections at the University of Washington and reading through newspaper clippings from the Seattle Public Library. Entering Sappho is an engagement with desperate, indulgent, and condescending nostalgia. It documents a wish for this special kind of small-town life.

Entering Sappho is placing the one town in the United States ever to receive this name among thousands of others memorializing ancient Greece and Rome. In 1967, Wilbur

Zelinsky tried to list them all, but he didn't include Sappho. He showed how these classically named towns extend from Western New York across the continent like an 'irregular scattering of open blotches, an advanced stage of a bacterial culture,' although he was entirely approving. The family who gave Sappho its name had followed a similar path across the time and space of the United States. Their last name was 'Lamoureux' – the lovers.

The settlers who founded the town were fond of Sappho's poetry. Entering Sappho is reading her work for its breathless excitement, its urge to overtake, its singular obsession with wanting. Entering Sappho is finding the tones, textures, and lines where greedy desire opens history – her poems recast the smitten and covetous descriptions of depopulated landscapes found in Ruby El Hult's *The Untamed Olympics* (1954) and everywhere else. What's important to me is that entering Sappho is specifically entering – it is a strategy explicitly opposed to getting out of it, to escaping blame. There is no exemption for being queer, for not being a man. You could write a book like this about almost any town in North America, but for me, Sappho is a point of obvious complicity. I got this book, *L'Égal des dieux*, which presents one hundred different translations of Poem 31, Sappho's jealousy poem, from Louise Labé (c. 1550s) to the contemporary moment. I started doing pseudo-translations from it, using those to connect different kinds of annihilating desire, what I saw in the awful archive and what I saw all around.

I think there is a risk in erasing all distinctions. But I also think people like me – white queer people – need to figure out which gestures we're repeating. The elaborately ritualistic European claims to the lands, seas, rivers, ports, gulfs, archipelagoes, and bays of the Pacific Northwest documented by

Jose Mariano Moziño in 1792 must also have been saturated with giddy excitement, in spite of their strict religious solemnity. Entering Sappho is an insistence that there is no getting out of, no getting past, even as short a history as Sappho's. But entering Sappho is also a tentative hope that just as Sappho is utterly transformed so too might our current condition be altered. Entering Sappho is a desperate wanting, it is work toward remaking, it is an unquenchable desire for something better and something beautiful.

'Clip' quotes extensively from Don Duncan's* *Seattle Times* article 'Yes, Virginia, there IS a Pysht' (1972). 'Oral History' quotes extensively from an interview with Guy Lashure, a settler from Sappho, WA, recorded by Jervis Russell in 1962. 'Soft Memory' is made up of pseudo-translations from numerous poems in the anthology *L'Égal des dieux: Cent versions d'un poème de Sappho*, edited by Philippe Brunet (Éditions Allia, 1998). 'This Word: I Want' quotes extensively from Wilbur Zelinsky's research article 'Classical Town Names in the United States: The Historical Geography of an American Idea' (1967), and Ruby El Hult's *The Untamed Olympics* (1954), a history of the Olympic Peninsula. 'US' quotes extensively from *Some Early Years in the Rain Forest* by Harvey Lamoureux, edited and illustrated by Kay Lamoureux Buckner (1979). 'These Things Now for My Companions / I Shall Sing Beautifully' quotes from José Mariano Moziño's *Noticias de Nutka* (1792), accessed through Iris H. Wilson Engstrand's 1991 edition, but offered here in my own pseudo-translation. Throughout the book, I draw phrases and images from a range of different versions of Sappho's poems, and from quotations attributed to Felix Gonzalez-Torres.

ABOUT THE AUTHOR

Sarah Dowling is the author of *DOWN*, and *Security Posture*, which received the Robert Kroetsch Award for Innovative Poetry. A literary critic as well as a poet, Sarah's first scholarly book, *Translingual Poetics: Writing Personhood under Settler Colonialism*, was a finalist for the American Studies Association's Lora Romero Prize. Sarah is an assistant professor in the Centre for Comparative Literature and Victoria College at the University of Toronto.

Typeset in Arno and Gibson

Printed at the old Coach House on bpNichol Lane in Toronto, Ontario, on Rolland Opaque Natural paper, which was manufactured, acid-free, in Saint-Jérôme, Quebec, from 50 percent recycled paper, and it was printed with vegetable-based ink on a 1972 Heidelberg KORD offset litho press. Its pages were folded on a Baumfolder, gathered by hand, bound on a Sulby Auto-Minabinda, and trimmed on a Polar single-knife cutter.

Edited by Susan Holbrook
Cover and interior design by Crystal Sikma
Author photo by Paul Terefenko

Coach House Books
80 bpNichol Lane
Toronto ON M5S 3J4
Canada

416 979 2217
800 367 6360

mail@chbooks.com
www.chbooks.com